# FABULOUS BEASTS

ALISON LURIE

Illustrated by
MONIKA BEISNER

JONATHAN CAPE
THIRTY BEDFORD SQUARE LONDON

*also by Alison Lurie and Monika Beisner*
The Heavenly Zoo

First published 1981
Illustrations copyright © 1981 by Monika Beisner
Text copyright © 1981 by Alison Lurie

Jonathan Cape Ltd, 30 Bedford Square, London WC1

British Library Cataloguing in Publication Data

Lurie, Alison
I. Title    II. Beisner, Monika
823´.914 [J]    PZ7

ISBN 0–224–01971–6

Printed in Italy by Amilcare Pizzi S.p.A., Milano

# *Preface*

IN THE PAST, many strange beasts and birds were thought to live in wild and distant parts of the world. Travellers brought back tales of flying horses, geese that grew on trees, lizards that could live in fire and many other wonders. Later most of these stories were explained as mistakes and exaggerations, or as confused recollections of long-extinct creatures: the Dragon, for instance, was said to be a memory of the last of the dinosaurs.

Is it really true that these wonderful beasts and birds never existed, or (if they once did) are now gone for ever? Even today people report seeing creatures just as strange in out-of-the-way places: the mountains of Tibet, the forests of the Canadian north-west, the depths of the ocean. Perhaps the Unicorn, the Griffin, the Roc and all the others in this book were real after all, and are still alive somewhere in the world. Perhaps some day, if you are lucky, you will see them.

NE OF THE rarest and most wonderful beasts on earth is the UNICORN. In appearance it is like a beautiful little white horse of the finest breed, but bearded like a goat. From the centre of its forehead grows a long spiral-patterned horn; hence, the name Uni-corn or "one-horn". It dwells in the forest and is sometimes seen browsing in flowery woodland meadows.

The horn of this beast has many marvellous properties. When a pool or stream has become muddied and foul, so that all the animals and birds of the forest avoid it, the Unicorn has only to dip in its horn for the water to become clear and sweet again. Cups and goblets made of Unicorn horn have the same purifying virtue. Ground into a powder, the horn cures fevers, fits and the plague. It makes drunken men sober, madmen wise, and is a certain antidote to all poisons.

In ancient times the only known means of catching a Unicorn was to flee from it towards a large tree, and then dodge aside at the last moment in the faint hope that the beast might run its horn into the trunk of the tree and be unable to escape.

Presently, however, a way was found not only to trap but to tame the Unicorn. A maiden would go into the woods or meadows where the beast was wont to graze and sit waiting. If a Unicorn scented her, it would come and lay its head in her lap. As she stroked its silky mane, it would fall asleep and the hunters could approach and capture it. Nor would it desire to flee as long as the maiden was near. In this way, the precious horn could be obtained without injuring the beast; for Unicorns may cast their horns in maturity and grow new ones.

THE BASILISK OR Cockatrice is the king of serpents, just as the lion is the king of beasts. It has the head and body of a cock, leathery spiked wings, and a long barbed serpent's tail. Sometimes it bears a crown or coronet upon its head in token of its royalty. According to certain writers, it comes forth out of a seven-year-old cock's egg. This egg is not white or brown like that of a hen, but yellow and lumpish; and it is said that the Basilisk is hatched either by the cock himself or by a toad, which may sit on the egg for up to nine years.

The Basilisk dwells in the Libyan desert, and also creates a desert wherever it goes. So poisonous is its breath that the grass scorches and blackens where it has passed, shrubs and trees wither and even the rocks split apart. Birds flying too low overhead are overcome and fall dead out of the sky. Indeed, the very glance of the Basilisk's red eyes is enough to kill, and travellers who see one from afar flee for their lives.

Fortunately, this terrible creature is terrified of three things. One is the weasel, which is immune to the Basilisk's poison and will attack it on sight. All Basilisks also fear the crowing of a true cock: they themselves can only hiss like serpents. Finally, they have a dread of mirrors; for if a Basilisk should look into a mirror even for a moment it would be struck dead by the sight of its own image.

HE SIMURGH, WHICH dwells high in the Persian mountains, is a large and beautiful bird with a dog's head; it has orange feathers that shine like polished copper, the talons of a vulture, and a tail like a peacock's. The Simurgh makes its nest in the branches of the Tree of Knowledge and is the wisest of all birds. It speaks all languages, and can tell what has been, what is and what will be.

The Persian poet Firdausi relates the story of how a Simurgh rescued the infant prince Zál, son of King Sám. When Zál was born his hair was as white as snow, and King Sám's fearful advisers said that the baby must be a demon. The King therefore had his son sent away into the mountains and left there to die.

A Simurgh flying overhead in search of food for her fledglings found Zál crying and carried him home to her nest. There she fed and cared for him and brought him up with her own children. Since she knew all things, she was able to educate the young prince in the history, geography, language and arts of Persia; she also taught him to hunt and fight and to understand philosophy.

When Zál was nearly grown, King Sám saw him in a dream. Taking this as a sign that the prince was still alive, he went into the mountains to search for him. As the King wandered about, calling his son's name and begging to be forgiven for his former cruelty and folly, the Simurgh heard him. She restored the boy to his father, and Zál lived to become a wise and brave ruler of his people.

THERE IS IN Europe and Asia a kind of SALAMANDER remarkable for the coldness of its body, which is like ice to the touch even on the warmest days. It resembles the common salamander, a small spotted lizard found in the American south-west and in Mexico, but is somewhat larger and elegantly patterned in green and yellow. Not only does it prefer a hot climate, its love of heat is so great that it actually lives in fire. The artist Benvenuto Cellini tells how when he was about five years old his father called him to look at a tiny Salamander playing among the burning coals; at the same time he gave little Benvenuto a blow on the head so that he would always remember this rare and wonderful sight.

The fire-dwelling Salamanders are much valued by alchemists. Those who attempt to transform baser metals into gold know that their work has succeeded when after forty-one days and nights a Salamander appears glowing red in the heart of the furnace.

According to some writers, the skins of Salamanders are made of a substance very like the mineral asbestos. Garments woven from it will not burn, and can be cleaned by passing them through a fire. The Emperor of India is said to have had a cloak made from the skins of a thousand Salamanders. It is also said that some Salamanders are dangerous to man, for they spit out a tasteless milky substance which makes hair fall out and leaves a white mark on the skin like leprosy. They may easily be killed, however, by sprinkling salt on their tails.

HE LARGEST BIRD ever seen on earth is the ROC of Madagascar and the Indian Ocean: its outspread wings measure fifty feet from tip to tip. The famous traveller Marco Polo says that a full-grown Roc is strong enough to lift an elephant. Indeed, some Rocs have been known to carry off two at a time, one in each claw. They soar high up over the mountainside and drop the elephants, which are smashed into pieces on the stones; the monstrous birds then fly down and devour them.

Sinbad the Sailor, whose adventures are related in *The Arabian Nights*, was once abandoned on a desert island. When he climbed a tree, he saw in the distance what seemed to be a large white domed building. He made his way to it and walked all round, but could find no entrance. Just then, as the sun was setting, the rosy sky was suddenly darkened as if by a thick cloud. Sinbad looked up and saw a bird the size of a ship in full sail swooping down towards him; he realized that this must be a Roc, and the domed building her egg.

Though frightened, Sinbad did not lose heart. When the Roc sat down upon her egg he crept nearer, then with his turban he tied himself to one of the bird's legs, which was as thick as the trunk of a palm tree. As soon as it was light next morning the Roc took wing. She flew very high, then descended so rapidly and roughly that Sinbad fainted away. When he came to his senses again he was on the mainland. Quickly he untied himself and escaped, and thus lived to have many more wonderful adventures.

HE VEGETABLE LAMB or Barometz is one of the oddest creatures ever discovered. Though it resembles a young sheep, and grazes upon grass like a sheep, yet it grows out of the earth from a seed. Farmers in the wilds of Tartary, where it is found, plant these seeds (which resemble those of melons) each spring. The Vegetable Lamb sprouts quickly and grows to a height of two or three feet, producing a fruit which looks exactly like a real lamb. The lamb remains attached to its stalk all its life, and browses upon the grass and herbs nearby. When it has eaten everything within reach it withers and dies.

This Vegetable Lamb is useful to the Tartars in many ways. Its flesh or pulp is delicious roasted, baked or grilled. Even more valuable is the fleece, which is far more white and soft than that of a true sheep. It can be spun and woven into a cloth which is not rough like wool, but fine and smooth as silk – yet, unlike silk, it can be washed easily with soap and water. Since this cloth closely resembles cotton, some believe that the Vegetable Lamb is related to the cotton plant.

Farmers who can get the seeds prefer the Vegetable Lamb to any other breed of sheep. A flock of them grazing in a green field or on a hillside is a pretty sight, and there is of course no danger of their straying away, so there is no need for a shepherd.

THE GRIFFIN OR Gryphon is a fierce and noble beast, half-lion and half-eagle. It has a body and tail like that of a lion, only eight times larger, joined to the head and wings of an eagle, but with pointed ears like a dog's. Its colour varies: some Griffins are dark-blue, with rose-red feathers on their breasts and white wings tipped with blue, whilst their bodies are tawny like a lion's. The Italian poet Dante, on his visit to Purgatory, saw a Griffin whose wings and head were of pure gold, and the rest white mixed with vermilion, so that he seemed to outshine the sun.

Griffins live in wild mountainous or desert country, making their nests on cliffs, from which they descend to the plains to hunt. Since each Griffin is stronger than a hundred eagles, it can easily carry off a pair of horses or two oxen yoked together. Other Griffins serve the gods as horses do men. Nemesis, the dreadful goddess whose task it is to pursue evil-doers and avenge crimes, always travels in a chariot drawn by these beasts.

The long claws of the Griffin, each of which is as large as the horn of an ox, darken at the touch of poison, and for this reason they are much sought after. Griffins are so fierce and vigilant that they cannot be captured or killed; but occasionally a holy man or woman who has retired to the wilderness will come upon one which has wounded itself on the rocks, or stepped on a thorn. If the hermit is brave and kind enough to heal the beast, the grateful Griffin will break off one of its claws as a reward. (In time, of course, the claw will grow again just as fingernails do.)

T HE SAVAGE GULON, which lives in the northern wilds of Sweden, is a beast about the size of a large dog, but with the face and ears of a cat. Its teeth and claws are long and sharp and it has a short bushy tail like that of a fox. Its coat is thick, soft and wonderfully patterned in black and brown like a damask cloth, each animal having its own design.

The nature of the Gulon is fierce and cunning, and it is of all beasts the most greedy for meat. It does not kill living creatures, but falls upon the carcasses of dead animals, birds and men, eating so much and so fast that its body swells up like a great fur balloon and it can hardly walk. It then searches for two trees growing close together and squeezes itself through the gap between them so that some of the food is discharged. Afterwards it returns to the carcass and eats still more, repeating the process until nothing is left but the bare bones.

Hunters in the northern forest eagerly pursue the Gulon. Though it is sought mostly for its skin, many other parts of the beast are valuable. The teeth are used by magicians in their spells, its fat cures sores and a powder ground from its paws is good against dizziness and ringing in the ears. Its guts may be made into strings for instruments; when played they produce a fierce, harsh, sad music which gives much pleasure to the melancholy Swedes.

Though the skins of the Gulon are greatly valued, so that they are desired above all others by the rich and powerful, yet wise men and women will avoid them. For it is known that those who wear the damasked skins of the Gulon become little by little fierce, cruel and greedy for the things of the world; yet however great their treasure, they are never satisfied or at peace.

THE PHOENIX IS the rarest and most beautiful of all birds. Reports agree that it is glorious to look upon: some say that it is made all of red gold; some that it is purple with a golden neck; while others claim that its body is plum-coloured and its tail azure, intermingled with long feathers of a rosy hue. It appears from this that either the Phoenix can change colour as it chooses, or that all men and women see it according to their own desires.

There is only one Phoenix, which lives upon air and is immortal. It dwells in Phoenicia on the eastern shore of the Mediterranean; but when it feels itself growing weary – which happens once every five hundred years – it flies west towards Egypt, to Heliopolis, the City of the Sun. There, in a tall palm tree, it builds a nest of sweet-smelling woods and spices. At dawn it sings a hymn to the sun; then it claps its wings together, setting fire to the nest, and is consumed in the flames. But even as the fire dies down the Phoenix rises again from its own ashes, young and strong and shining. It rests for three days, then spreads its wings and flies eastward back to Phoenicia.

THE MIMICK DOG is one of the cleverest of known creatures, and has a wit surpassing that of most humans. It can easily be taught to jump, dance in time to music and play many tricks; and of its own accord will imitate all manner of beasts and men. In appearance it is rather homely, being somewhat like a small shaggy dog and somewhat like a monkey, with a short stumpy tail and a sharp long-nosed muzzle. Its expression is one of intelligent curiosity.

Mimick Dogs originally come from Egypt, where they were common in the time of King Ptolemy and were sometimes employed in poor men's houses instead of servants. Players also kept them to perform on the stage and in puppet shows. In Rome, a Mimick Dog once appeared before the Emperor Vespasian. It perfectly imitated the voices and actions of various sorts of dogs and other beasts, and finally pretended to die and revive with such skill that the Emperor and the rest of the company were charmed and amazed.

Today Mimick Dogs are more rare, but if you happen to meet one of them you are sure to be agreeably entertained as long as you treat it with respect and consideration. Indeed, to do otherwise is risky. If you are rude and unkind enough to sneer at a Mimick Dog because of its small size and untidy appearance, you may be followed by the creature you have insulted through the street, and even into your home, school or place of work. All day long the Mimick Dog will tag after you, mocking your walk, gestures and conversation in such a comic manner that no one who sees it will be able to help laughing at you.

IN THE HIGH plains and desert country of Africa near the sources of the Nile there dwells a sad and strange beast called the CATOBLEPAS which resembles a small, winged buffalo and eats only poisonous plants and weeds, those which would be fatal to other animals. It has a curly tail and is covered all over with scales like a dragon. Its large head is so heavy that the Catoblepas cannot lift it, but must drag it along the ground. Moreover, the beast can never look up because of the mane of stiff bristly hair that covers its face. According to some writers, this is just as well, for any living creature the Catoblepas gazed directly upon would fall dead instantly.

However, there is no record of anyone ever being slain by the glance of the Catoblepas. One is reported to have spoken threateningly to St Anthony during his stay in the desert; but perhaps this Catoblepas was simply annoyed at having been disturbed by the saint's loud prayers and lamentations, for it is a timid beast that loves solitude and quiet.

THE TREE GOOSE or Clayk grows upon trees on the shore of the island of Pomonia, to the north of Scotland. These trees, which look much like willows, produce large green fruits the size of melons. When the fruit is ripe, it falls into the sea and out of it hatches a living goose, which is red and pink in colour. For a little while these Tree Geese float upon the foamy waves near the shores; then they spread their wings and fly away over the ocean.

Those fruits that fall upon the land do not turn into geese, but they are said to be edible and tasty. The flesh of the Tree Goose itself is excellent when boiled or roasted. Though no one has been able to agree whether it is fruit, fish or fowl, it often used to be eaten during Lent.

THE DRAGON IS compounded of earth, air and fire: it crawls upon the ground like a lizard, flies like a bird and breathes out flames and smoke. Dragons are found in all parts of the world and come in many sizes, from little ones that live under stones and hiss like tea-kettles to terrible monsters larger than a house. Some crawl upon two legs and some upon four, and they may have one, three or even seven or nine heads. They may be of any colour, but the most common sort have glittering green scales and leathery red wings.

Certain Dragons are mild-tempered and friendly. Most, however, are fierce, cruel, treacherous and greedy. Many old Dragons have gathered great heaps of gold upon which they sleep, with one eye always half-open to watch for thieves. Whoever finds this treasure is best advised to spend it or give it away at once, for Dragon's gold casts an evil spell over its owner, and those who hoard it will slowly but surely turn into Dragons themselves.

The larger Dragons generally live in caves in mountainous or desolate places. From there they fly down to the nearby villages to carry off cattle, sheep and humans. Their favourite prey is young maidens, especially princesses. When a country is thus plagued, it must be proclaimed far and wide that whoever can kill the Dragon will be rewarded with half the kingdom and the princess's hand in marriage. Sooner or later the right hero will appear.

A dead Dragon, besides being a relief to the country, is useful in many ways. Its blood is prized by alchemists; its eyes, when dried and powdered, will cure nightmares; and its teeth, if planted with the proper incantations, will spring up overnight as armed men.

HE WINGED HORSE PEGASUS was created by Poseidon, the Greek god of the sea and of dreams. He was first caught and tamed by Athena, the goddess of wisdom, who presented him to the Muses, the nine patronesses of poetry, art and science. Pegasus is one of the most beautiful and noble creatures on earth, and can be ridden only by a hero or by a true poet: for only such men and women have both great visions and the power to understand them and make them come true.

The first hero to ride Pegasus was a Greek youth called Bellerophon, who was sent by the King of Lycia to slay a monster called the Chimera. This terrible beast breathed fire and had three heads: one like a lion, one like a goat and one like a snake. She lived in the mountains of Lycia and descended each day to the plain to devour people and cattle.

Before he set out to meet the Chimera, Bellerophon prayed to Athena for help. The goddess appeared to him in a dream and gave him a golden bridle, which he found in his hand when he awoke. Bellerophon searched through the forest for Pegasus; when he found him drinking from a spring he slipped the golden bridle over his head and was able to mount on his back. The great winged horse carried him up over the mountains to the cave of the Chimera. When she saw them, the monster roared like a lion, lashed her serpent's tail and breathed out smoke and flames, but Pegasus rose up in the air and escaped them; then he plunged back down as swiftly as the wind so that his rider might pierce the Chimera to the heart with his spear. Thus Bellerophon destroyed the monster, saved the Lycian people and married the daughter of their king.